The Ten Commandments

Pocket Guide

* * *

William Barclay

Westminster John Knox Press
Louisville, Kentucky

Designed by
ANDREW MILNE DESIGN

Published in 2001 by
WESTMINSTER JOHN KNOX PRESS
Louisville, Kentucky

Printed in Hong Kong

01 02 03 04 05 06 07 08 09 00 — 10 9 8 7 6 5 4 3 2 1

A catalog card for this book may be obtained from the
Library of Congress.

ISBN 0-664-22346-X

Contents

INTRODUCTION

The Ancient Foundation

C hristianity did not come into this world without
roots and foundations. The Christian Ethic had a
foundation. Jesus did not come into a society which
knew nothing of goodness and of morality and of
ethics and of God. He came into a society which
already possessed the Law *(Matthew 5:17)*.

UNIVERSAL FOUNDATION

The Jewish ethic was itself founded on the Ten
Commandments. Theses might well be called the universal
foundation, not only of Jewish ethics, but of all ethics.
They contain the basic laws of human conduct in society.

I This code has two sections

This code falls quite clearly into two sections. The first
section deals with God, and the seconddeals with man.

A. THE DIVINE SECTION

- ❖ The lonely supremacy of God is laid down.
- ❖ The impossibility of expressing God in any material
  form is stated.
- ❖ The reckless use of the name of God in promises
  and pledges is forbidden.
- ❖ The right use of God's day are safe-guarded.

B. The human section

- ❖ Father and mother are to be honored.
- ❖ Human life is sacred.
- ❖ Sexual purity and fidelity are demanded.
- ❖ The rights of human property are conserved.
- ❖ False speaking about others is condemned.
- ❖ The desire for that which is not ours and which is not for us is branded as wrong.

II This code is a series of principles

The second thing to note about the Ten Commandments is that they are a series of principles, and not a body of detailed rules and regulations. The Ten Commandments say: "Here is how you ought to feel towards God and towards man. In each separate situation work out the expression in action of that feeling for yourself."

III This code is stated in the form of negatives

The commonest criticism of the Ten Commandments is that they are a series of "Thou shalt nots". But for a mob of people who escaped from Egypt to become a nation they must have a law which they will obey and which will weld them into a community. The Ten Commandments are the law without which nationhood is impossible. That is why the Ten Commandments are largely negative.

> ### REVERENCE AND RESPECT
>
> *It may be said that this code inculcates two basic things — it demands reverence for God and respect for man.*

CHAPTER ONE

The First Commandment

> "YOU SHALL HAVE NO
> OTHER GODS
> BEFORE ME"
>
> ──────────────
>
> EXODUS 20:3

THE ONLY GOD

I Stage one: Polytheism

Men's belief about God passed through three stages. The
first stage was polytheism, which means the belief in many
gods. At that stage men believed in a whole host of gods.
They believed in:

- ❖ a god of the sun
- ❖ a god of the moon
- ❖ a god of the sea
- ❖ a god of the sky

❖ a god of the fire
❖ a god of the wind
❖ a god of the river
❖ a god of the mountain
❖ and a god of the wood

The world at this stage was crammed with gods and goddesses, competing, as it were, for the gifts and the worship of men.

II Stage two: Henotheism

The second stage was henotheism. At this stage a nation would accept one god as its god and would worship no other; but it was quite prepared to believe that the gods of the other nations were as real as its own god. At this stage a god was, as it were, supreme within its own territory, but other territories had other gods. At this stage a conflict between nations was a conflict between their gods, because the territory of the nation and the territory of the god were co-extensive *(see Judges 11:24)*.

III Stage three: Monotheism

The last and final stage is monotheism, and this is the belief that there is not simply one god for each nation, but that there is only one God for all the earth. This is the belief of the Psalmist who thinks of the God whose presence fills the whole world and the uttermost parts of the earth and of the sea, and from whom even death could not separate him *(Psalm 139:1-12)*.

If a man left his god behind him when he left his native land, his religion was but a broken reed; and especially in the bitter days of the exile the people of Israel had to learn to think of God as with them not just in Palestine but even in the distant and strange lands.

ONE GOD

So then the Jews came in the end to believe in one God.
In the Revised Standard Version this first commandment is
given in two forms, *"You shall have no other gods before me,"*
and in the margin, *"You shall have no other gods besides me."*
The first form is henotheism, the form in which Jahweh
was the God for Israel, although there were other gods for
other nations; the second form is monotheism, the belief
that there is no other god besides Jahweh at all.

THE DANGER OF BAAL WORSHIP

BELIEF SHAPES BEHAVIOR

It might be thought that to begin like this is to begin
with theology rather than with ethics, but theology and
ethics cannot be separated. It is necessary to begin with
God, for the very simple reason that, if men believe in
gods at all, they will necessarily wish to be like the gods in
whom they believe, and, therefore, the kind of gods they
believe in will make all the difference to the kind of life
which they live.

BAAL WORSHIP

In the Old Testament it is plain that the prophets regarded
Baal worship as a very serious and dangerous threat to the
purity of religion.

The basic idea of Baal worship was this. The most
mysterious force in life is growth. What makes the corn
grow, and the grape swell, and the olive ripen? That, said
the other nations, is Baal or the Baals at work. Baal is the
power of growth behind all living and growing things. But
it was God not Baal who was behind this wonderful

growth, see *Hosea 2:8*, but there were many who worshiped the Baals and forgot God.

ONLY ONE GOD

That is why the Ten Commandments begin by insisting that there is only one God, and all these other so-called gods are false imposters.

So then we come back to the point with which we started. It is of the first necessity to get the idea of God right, for a man will quite inevitably become like the god he worships.

MAN BECOMES LIKE THE GOD HE WORSHIPS

If he worships a licentious god like the Baals he will become a licentious man.

If he worships a hard stern god, then he will, as the world has so often tragically seen, become a hard stern man.

If he worships a sentimentalized god, he will have a sentimentalized idea of religion.

It is from here that ethics takes its start. A man's god dictates a man's conduct, consciously or unconsciously.

> ### THE IMITATION OF CHRIST
>
> *The Christian believes in the God who is the God and Father of our Lord Jesus Christ, the God whose mind and heart and character is seen in the life and death of Jesus. And for that very reason the Christian Ethic might well be said to be the imitation of Christ.*

CHAPTER TWO

The Second Commandment

> "YOU SHALL NOT MAKE FOR YOURSELF A GRAVEN IMAGE"
>
> EXODUS 20:4

THE INVISIBLE GOD

The second commandment is the prohibition of the making or the worshiping of an idol.

AN IDOL IS A PARADOXICAL THING

I An idol is nothing

In one sense there is nothing more unnatural and even more ridiculous than an idol.

JEREMIAH'S VIEW OF IDOLS

The idol is there, incapable of movement, fixed to the one place as fast as a scarecrow in a cucumber field *(Jeremiah 10:3-5)*. From one point of view it is incredible that a man should regard as a god that which he himself cut and carved, that which he has to carry about like unwieldy baggage. It seems unnatural to regard a thing like that as in any sense divine.

10

II An idol is regarded as divine

On the other hand it is easy to
understand the process by which an
idol comes to be regarded as divine.
God is unseen, a spirit and a power
invisible to men. It is very hard for
simple people to remember, to think
about and to worship, an unseen god.
Well, then, let us try to make it a little
easier for people.

TODAY'S MEANING OF IDOLATRY

I Idolatry means making means into ends

A LITURGY

A liturgy is a means of worshiping God; but an elaborate
liturgy can become an end in itself, becoming more
important than the worship itself.

A CHURCH BUILDING

A church building is a means whereby a group of people
can worship God; but people can end up worshiping the
building, more concerned with the place of worship than
the worship itself.

II Idolatry substitutes the thing for the person

The essence of idolatry is that it is the worship of a thing
instead of a person; the dead idol has taken the place of
the living God.

> ### ISAIAH'S VIEW OF IDOLS
>
> *Isaiah pours scorn on the
> man who makes an idol. He
> takes a piece of wood and
> with one bit of it he makes
> a fire to warm himself; with
> another bit of it he makes a
> fire to cook his dinner; and
> with a third bit of it he
> makes a god.*
>
> (ISAIAH 44:14-20)

CHAPTER THREE

The Third Commandment

> "YOU SHALL NOT TAKE
> THE NAME OF THE
> LORD YOUR GOD
> IN VAIN"
>
> EXODUS 20:7

IN THE NAME OF GOD

In the *Authorized Version* the third commandment runs: *"Thou shalt not take the name of the Lord thy God in vain"* (Exodus 20:7) and apart from altering the thou to you the Revised Standard Version is the same.

WHAT DOES "IN VAIN" MEAN?

❖ In Hebrew the phrase literally means for unreality.
❖ It is often translated in the AV as vanity.
❖ The word means empty, insincere, frivolous.

This commandment forbiots the use of God's name in an empty, frivolous or insincere way.

PROMISES, PROMISES

This commandment lays down the sanctity of promises. Let us look at all the promises we make.

The ordinary promises and undertakings of life: but life is littered with broken promises.

The promise in every contract of work. Our employer undertakes to give us so much money; we undertake to give him our work.

There is the promise in the law courts, before God by name, to tell the truth, the whole truth and nothing but the truth – an oath broken daily.

There is the marriage vow for which we will answer to God.

The pledge of baptism in which parents pledge to bring up a child in the knowledge, love and the fear of God.

The pledge of the sacrament. When a man must renew his oath of loyalty to Christ as his Savior and King.

In a pledge or in a promise

The commandment is a prohibition of taking the name of God in vain in a promise or a pledge, that is, of making such a promise or pledge in the name of God with no intention of keeping it, or of making a promise in the name of God and then afterwards breaking it because it was inconvenient or uncomfortable.

CHAPTER FOUR

The Fourth Commandment

> ## "REMEMBER THE SABBATH DAY TO KEEP IT HOLY"
>
> EXODUS 20:8

GOD'S DAY AND HOW TO USE IT

Set out in full the fourth commandment runs: *"Remember the sabbath day, to keep it holy. Six days you shall labor, and do all your work; but the seventh day is a sabbath to the Lord your God; in it you shall not do any work, you, or your son, or your daughter, your manservant, or your maidservant, or your cattle, or the sojourner who is within your gates; for in six days the Lord made heaven and earth, the sea, and all that is in them, and rested the seventh day; therefore the Lord blessed the sabbath day and hallowed it." (Exodus 20:8-11)*

HUMANITARIAN LEGISLATION

As it stands this commandment is primarily a great piece of social and humanitarian legislation. It is not primarily a religious regulation at all. What is laid down is a day of rest on which even the serving men and women lay aside

their tasks and on which even the
toiling beasts are not forgotten, and
when even the stranger and foreigner
share in this rest.

THE DAY OF THE RESURRECTION

There are signs that in the New
Testament itself the first day of the
week, the day of the Resurrection, is
becoming the Christian day.

> ## FOR THE JEW
>
> *For the Jew the Sabbath was
> the last day of the seven-day
> week, the day on which God
> rested after the work of
> creation, and the essential
> way of keeping the Sabbath
> was for man to rest as God
> had rested.*

The Sabbath is not listed as one of
the basic things which Gentile
Christians must accept and observe
(Acts 15:20, 29).

On the first day of the week the congregation met to
break bread at Troas *(Acts 20:7)*.

On the first day of the week the Corinthians put
something aside for the Jerusalem Church
(1 Corinthians 16:2).

FROM THE JEWISH SABBATH TO THE LORD'S DAY

The Jewish Sabbath had tended to become a day of
restrictions and prohibitions observed in a legalistic spirit.

Paul's view

Now it is clear that to one man at least any such day
would be the reverse of the whole Christian gospel, and
that man was Paul. And we do in fact find Paul:

- ❖ Condemning those who observe days and months
  and seasons and years *(Galatians 4:10)*.
- ❖ Insisting that Christians must not get involved
  in questions about festivals and new moons and
  Sabbaths *(Colossians 2:16)*.

❖ Holding that the man who is really strong in the faith will require no special holy days at all, but will regard all days as holy *(Romans 14:5, 6)*.

We may take it as certain in Paul's churches there would be a strong move away from the legalistic Sabbath towards a Resurrection joy of the Lord's Day.

KEEPING THE SABBATH

Every time we become involved in arguments about what may or may not be done on the Lord's Day we are, in fact, being Jewish instead of Christian, and we are, in fact, turning the Lord's Day into the Sabbath again.

The Sabbath is not a Christian institution, the Lord's Day is.

This fourth commandment is not binding on the Christian at all, for there is no evidence in Scripture that the rules and regulations which govern the Sabbath were ever transferred by divine authority to the Lord's Day.

I Ought we to keep the Lord's Day?

How shall we keep the Lord's Day? The prior question is: Ought we to observe and keep any special day at all?

It was clearly Paul's point of view that the really strong Christian would observe all days alike *(Romans 14:1-6)*.

But he also knew human nature well enough to know that to observe all days alike would in all probability mean to observe none at all. In theory we can argue that no special day is necessary and all days are God's days, but in practice we need a special day on which to focus our thoughts on God and on our risen Lord.

II What is the purpose of this day?

In the first instance, a day of rest is still a necessity. As the

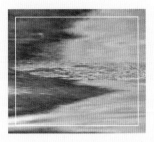

old Greek proverb had it, the bow that is always bent (that is, always stretched taut) will soon cease to shoot straight.

A day of rest is a social and industrial necessity without which health and work inevitably suffer.

WHAT IS REST?

When the commandment itself was laid down, it was laid down in a society where almost all work was physical work. A man tilled the soil, or reaped the harvest, or fished in the lake, or watched the flock. He would come to the end of the week with aching muscles and a body exhausted.

But the modern situation is quite different. There is much less work which is purely physical, and there is much more work which is done with more or less no physical effort at all. For the man in this situation a day of rest will be a day when he actively uses his body, and by so doing preserves his health.

And for that very reason no man need have a guilty conscience if on the Lord's Day he plays some healthy game, or swims in the sea, or climbs the hills, or walks in the country.

III The Lord's Day will be a family day
No faith sets a higher value on the family than
Christianity does.

<small>ANCIENT DAYS AND MODERN CONDITIONS</small>

In the ancient times the family did live together on the
farm and in the fishing boat and in the village. Day and
daily they lived, worked, ate and slept together.

But in modern conditions it can happen that the
members of the family rarely see each other through the
week. When the children grow up and marry, they do not
stay in the old home; they leave it and go their own ways.

In such circumstances the Lord's Day can be, and
ought to be:

- ✦ The family meeting day, the day when members of
  the family meet as a family.
- ✦ The day when sons and daughters who have gone
  out come back home again.
- ✦ The day when the grandchildren meet their
  grandparents.
- ✦ The day when the family circle, so interrupted and
  broken by modern life, comes together again.

IV The Lord's Day was always the day when God's people met and assembled together
If we can work out the reasons why they did meet
together, then we will go far towards finding the most
important uses of the Lord's Day.

The way in which we can best do this is by going
back to the early Church, and setting down that Church's
own description of the meeting together of the
Christians.

I They used the Lord's Day for study

Both Justin and Tertullian stress the reading of Scripture.

II They used the Lord's Day for prayer

On the Lord's Day they took life and laid it before God. If the Lord's Day is nothing else, it must be the day when we stop and remember God.

III They used the Lord's Day for fellowship

It was on that day, week by week, that they had their Love Feast, to which they came together in a togetherness which overcame all social barriers.

IV They used the Lord's Day to make that fellowship practically different

Part of the unvarying pattern is the voluntary offering for those in trouble and need. Today that may well be best done by visiting someone who is old or lonely.

V They used the Lord's Day for praise

Paul speaks about the man who comes to the Church's worship with a hymn *(1 Corinthians 14:26)*.

> #### Sunday lunch
>
> *Even to this day there is a certain symbolism in the Sunday midday meal. It can become a kind of sacrament of the home.*

V The Lord's Day should be used for worship

The word worship is a very wide word.

Worship is:

❖ Worth-ship.

❖ To confess and experience the supreme worth of God.

❖ The means to find the presence of God, and through that discovery to find inspiration and the strength to live a life which is fit for the presence of God.

WILLIAM TEMPLE

William Temple's definition of worship places worship in the wider context which it ought to have. "To worship," Temple wrote, *"is:*

to quicken the conscience by the holiness of God

to feed the mind withethe truth of God

to purge the imagination by the beauty of God

to open the heart to the love of God

to devote the will to the purpose of God."

MANY WAYS TO WORSHIP

We must clearly and willingly admit that there are many ways to worship. However difficult it is for the conventional religious mind to recognize it or admit it, the Church is not the only place in which worship in the real sense of the word is possible.

MUSIC

A man can worship in music. When Handel was asked how he had

succeeded in writing the music of his Messiah, he answered: *"I saw the Heavens open, and God sitting on the great white throne,"* and it is just that same experience that music can bring to some.

Nature

There are those for whom nature itself is the cathedral of God. Wordsworth writes of this experience of nature in "Lines composed a few miles above Tintern Abbey".

> *I have felt*
> *A presence that disturbs me with the joy*
> *Of elevated thoughts; a sense sublime*
> *Whose dwelling is the light of setting suns,*
> *And the round ocean and the living air,*
> *And the blue sky, and in the mind of man.*

There is no doubt that this is a description of worship, and unquestionably a man can worship in nature; it would be strange if we could not meet God in the world that God has made.

THE LORD'S DAY IS:

- ❖ *Not* the Jewish Sabbath.
- ❖ A day of rest, but rest must be interpreted according to the needs of the individual.
- ❖ The day of the meeting of families and friends.
- ❖ The day when we seek to enter more deeply, in learning, in reading, in study, in discussion into the meaning of the faith.
- ❖ The day when we remember those who are lonely and in need.
- ❖ The day when in worship we realize the presence of God in order to go out and to walk in it through all the days of the week.

CHAPTER FIVE

The Fifth
Commandment

"HONOR YOUR FATHER
AND YOUR MOTHER"

EXODUS 20:12

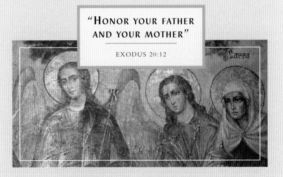

FATHER AND MOTHER

EXODUS AND LEVITICUS

This commandment is built into the very structure of
human society. It occurs again in a slightly different form
in *Leviticus 19:3*: *"Every one of you shall revere his mother and
his father."*

The Jewish rabbis with their passion for detailed
exegesis of Scripture were not slow to note that in the
Exodus version the father comes first, and in the Leviticus
version the mother comes first, and they used this to

prove that the honor to father and to mother must be the same. The double form of the commandment, so the rabbis argued, existed to make sure that the same honor was given to father and to mother.

PENALTIES

The sternest penalties were threatened against the person who broke this commandment. Everyone who curses his father or his mother shall be put to death *(Leviticus 20:9; Exodus 21:17)*.

> *"If one curses his father or his mother, his lamp will be put out in utter darkness" (Proverbs 20:20). "The eye that mocks a father and scorns to obey a mother will be picked out by the ravens of the valley, and eaten by the vultures" (Proverbs 30:17).*

No one is left in any doubt about the seriousness of breaking this commandment.

HOW MUST THE CHILD HONOR THE PARENT?

I Gratitude

Gratitude will be a necessary part of honor for parents. It is literally true that the child owes the parent his life in a double sense of the term. He owes him his life through birth, but he also owes him his life in that the parent cared for him and provided for him in the day and years when he could not care and provide for himself, and when, if he had been left to himself, he would certainly have perished.

II Obedience

Obedience will be a necessary part of honor for parents. It is but natural that the child should obey the parent. The child must believe that the parent's love will never ask him to do anything but what is for his good.

But a parent must earn the right to be obeyed. He can never resort to the method of the dictator and the tyrant and say: "Do it because I say it."

III Support

Support will be a necessary part of honor for parents. The child will wish to see that the parent in his old age or weakness does not lack for the necessities of life and is never either in need or in loneliness.

How must the parent honor the child?

Duty is never in the Christian Ethic one-sided, it is always a reciprocal obligation. And in this case, this is to say that there is a very real sense in which the parent must honor the child, just as the child must honor the parent.

I There is the basic duty of nourishment, care and support

When Christianity came into the world, child exposure was a normal custom, carrying with it no discredit and no stigma, and certainly not regarded as a crime.

II There is the basic duty of training and discipline

The parent owes it to the child to bring him up in such a way that he will become a responsible citizen.

The circular opposite was once issued by the police department of Houston, Texas.

III Encouragement

But there is another side to this. Certainly the parent must give the child discipline, but equally certainly the parent must give the child encouragement.

How to make a child into a Delinquent:

12 EASY RULES

1. Begin at infancy to give the child everything he wants. In this way he will grow up to believe that the world owes him a living.

2. When he picks up bad words laugh at him. This will make him think he's cute.

3. Never give him any spiritual training. Wait until he is twenty-one and then let him decide for himself.

4. Avoid the use of the word 'wrong'. The child may develop a guilt complex. This will condition him to believe later, when arrested for stealing a car, that society is against him and that he's being persecuted.

5. Pick up everything he leaves lying around, books, shoes, clothes. Do everything for him so that he will be experienced in throwing all responsibility on other people.

6. Let him read any printed material he can get his hands on. Be careful that his silver wear and drinking glasses are sterilized, but let his mind feed on garbage.

7. Quarrel frequently in the presence of your children. In this way they will not be too shocked when the home is broken up later.

8. Give a child all the spending money he wants. Never let him earn his own. Why should he have things as tough as you had them?

9. Satisfy every craving for food, drink and comfort. See that every sensual desire is satisfied. Denial may lead to harmful frustration.

10. Take his part against neighbours, teachers, policemen. They are all prejudicial against your child.

11. When he gets into real trouble apologize for him yourself by saying, I never could do anything with him.'

12. Prepare for a life of grief. You will be likely to have it.

PAUL'S INSTRUCTION

"Fathers," said Paul, "do not provoke your children, less they become discouraged" (Colossians 3:21). Or, as the New English Bible has it: "Fathers, do not exasperate your children, for fear they grow disheartened."

BENGEL'S COMMENT

Bengel's comment on this is that what Paul is warning against is that which produces *"the bane of youth, a broken spirit"*. There is a discipline which drives to despondency rather than to new and greater effort.

Luther hesitated to give the name father to God, because his own father had been so stern and severe with him.

IV There is the duty of sympathetic understanding

There are too many homes in which parents and children are almost strangers to each other.

The biggest step towards sympathetic understanding will come quite simply from the realization that we cannot expect our children to be the same as ourselves. It should be easier for those of us who are older than it is for youth out of our maturity to exercise the patience which will keep open the lines of communication between the generations.

V Respect

The parent must give the child the respect that is due to a person.

* ❖ The parent of the clever and the precocious child may look on the child as something to be exhibited.
* ❖ The parent of the spoilt and petulant child may look on the child as someone to be directed and controlled.

The only true way to look at any human being is as a person to be respected.

The way to respect a person is to treat him as an intelligent human being.

- ❖ Make life a partnership.
- ❖ Learn together.
- ❖ Ask for reasonable co-operation instead of blind obedience.
- ❖ Always be ready to explain why.
- ❖ Respect the child as we ourselves would wish to be respected.

VI Love

All that we have been saying can be summed up in the simple truth that what the parent must give to the child above all is love.

This is why even a not-so-good home where there is love is better than a sterilized, antiseptic, hygienic institution where there is no love. All the techniques and all the medical and psychological perfection in the world will not replace a mother's love, and that is not a sentimental statement — it is a fact.

The parent-child relationship must be a relationship of love. If that is there, nothing else is needed; and if it is not there literally nothing can replace it.

CHAPTER SIX

The Sixth Commandment

> ## "YOU SHALL NOT KILL"
> ---
> EXODUS 20:13

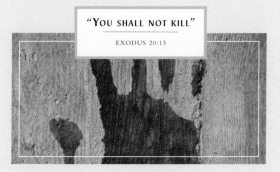

LIFE IS SACRED

MURDER OR KILLING IN GENERAL?

In the RSV and the AV the sixth commandment reads: *"You shall not kill" (Exodus 20:13)*, but the modern versions in general substitute the word murder for kill; and so in Moffatt and Goodspeed and the RV the commandment forbids murder specifically, and not killing in general.

This is correct, for in the Hebrew the verb implies, as Driver puts it, *"violent and unauthorized killing"*.

A DEPRAVED SOCIETY

Disobedience to this commandment is the sign of a depraved society. It is the complaint of Hosea: *"There is no faithfulness or kindness, and no knowledge of God in the land; there is swearing, lying, killing, stealing, committing adultery; they break all bounds and murder follows murder" (Hosea 4:1, 2).*

Jeremiah hears the condemnation of God to the people: *"Will you steal, murder, commit adultery, swear falsely, burn incense to Baal, and go after other gods that you have not known, and then come and stand before me in this house ...?" (Jeremiah 7:9).*

THE IMAGE OF GOD

Since man is made in the image of God *(Genesis 9:6),* then the taking of a single life is the destruction of the most precious and the most holy thing in the world. This commandment in itself needs no defense. It carries its eternal validity on its face.

But out of this ancient commandment there arise three very controversial issues for modern ethics and for modern society.

CAPITAL PUNISHMENT

First, there is the question: What is the bearing of this commandment on capital punishment? Is the killing of a man ever justified, even in the interests of legitimate punishment and social justice?

JEWISH BACKGROUND

Within the Jewish legal system it was never even suggested that this commandment forbade what may be called judicial killing. In point of fact, the death penalty was exacted for many crimes under Jewish law including:

- ❖ Murder *(Exodus 21:12)*.
- ❖ Child sacrifice *(Leviticus 20:2)*.
- ❖ Manslaughter *(Numbers 35:9-28)*.
- ❖ Keeping an ox known to be dangerous *(Exodus 21:29)*.
- ❖ Bearing false witness on a capital charge *(Deuteronomy 19:18-21)*.
- ❖ Kidnaping or stealing a man *(Exodus 21:16)*.
- ❖ Insult or injury to parents *(Exodus 21:15, 17)*.
- ❖ Various forms of sexual immorality *(Leviticus 18:6-18)*.
- ❖ Various religious and ritual offences, from witchcraft *(Exodus 22:18)* to Sabbath-breaking *(Exodus 31:14)*.

CARRYING OUT THE DEATH PENALTY

In the Tractate on the Sanhedrin in the Mishnah four ways of carrying out sentence are listed and described. They were: stoning, burning, beheading and strangling.

In practice, however, the mercy of Jewish law made it next to impossible to carry out the death penalty.

PUNISHMENT IN GENERAL

Before we can answer the question: Ought the death penalty to be retained in a Christian country? we must look at the aim of punishment?

I Society is built on law

Law is the foundation of society. Even in the ordinary everyday activities of life, such as motoring, house-building, buying and selling, the law is essential, if life is to go on at all. But human nature being what it is, there will always be the desire to break the law. So punishment and law go hand in hand.

II Restoration and restitution

If a crime has caused loss or injury to someone, there must be restoration and

restitution to conserve the interests of the person
wronged.

III Deterrent

Punishment is necessary as a deterrent, to demonstrate to
anyone contemplating crime that crime does not pay.

IV Punishment and the criminal

It must be a first principle of all Christian punishment
that it is not only for the sake of society, but that it is also
for the sake of the criminal. The one essential additional
element in the Christian view of punishment is that it
must always be remedial.

V Prevention

Prevention is always better than cure. It is our task as
Christians citizens to build a society in which crime will
lose its attraction. The extraordinary blindness of planners
who built housing schemes with literally no recreational
facilities is incomprehensible and unpardonable. The
energy which might have been employed in kicking a ball
is employed in heaving a brick through a window.

To take the remedial view of punishment means the
building up of an environment in which healthy activity
will take the place of criminal action, if it is not already in
many places too late.

EUTHANASIA

Out of the sixth commandment with its prohibition on killing there further arise two related questions to which the Christian answer must be decided. The first of these questions is, What is the Christian attitude to euthanasia?

WHAT IS EUTHANASIA?

Euthanasia is the doctrine which believes that when a person's life has become intolerable, when it may be argued that life is worse than death, then that life may be legitimately taken away.

- ❖ According to this belief a person who is suffering from some incurable and agonizing disease might be killed, kindly and humanely and presumably with his own consent, if he is still able to give consent.
- ❖ Or, this belief might argue, a child born deformed and obviously quite unable ever to live in the real sense might never be allowed to grow up.
- ❖ Or, it might be held, a child mentally and incurably deficient might be deprived of life before life ever really begins.

GREAT HESITATION

There are, however, good practical reasons as well as religious reasons for regarding euthanasia with the greatest hesitation.

I Defining the area

There is a very real difficulty of defining the area in which euthanasia might be practiced. Just when does a person reach that stage when it would be better for him to have his life ended? How is the word incurable to be defined? It would be a task to baffle human skill to decide at just what stage of human suffering or human abnormality a person becomes a fit subject for euthanasia.

II Who is to decide?
Who would take the decision as to the ending of the person's life? Would the relatives have the say? Would the person's own doctor decide? What part in the decision would the person himself have?

III Who takes the action?
Who would be responsible for the carrying out of the decision? Who would carry out what in law was a kind of justifiable homicide? Legally to saddle anyone with this responsibility would be an impossibility.

IV Scope for abuse
Any such scheme would without any doubt lend itself to enormous abuse. Once allowed, the right to take life under any circumstances may at any time be fabricated or unduly extended.

It is wrong
Apart from any of these practical difficulties there still remains the deep-seated conviction that it is basically wrong to give anyone the power of life and death

It is legally indefensible, practically impossible, morally wrong, and theologically unjustifiable.

· SUICIDE

The second of the questions which emerge from this commandment is: What is the Christian attitude to suicide? In the Bible euthanasia does not appear at all. In the Bible suicide appears as an event in both Testaments, but there is no definite teaching about it.

THREE SUMMARY THOUGHTS

I Unsound mind

We may well say that suicide always occurs when a man is of unsound mind. H.J. Rose has written: *"It is questionable whether any one whose life is of normal length is absolutely sane during every waking moment of it."*

And in suicide a man is, it may well be, always over the edge, for, as Schopenhauer say, suicide is the loss of will to live, and suicide is the denial that self-preservation is the first law of life. No one who commits suicide is in that moment of normal mind.

THOMAS AQUINAS

Thomas Aquinas forbade suicide on three grounds.

First, it is unnatural.

Second, it is a crime against the community.

Third, it is a usurpation of the prerogative of God, who alone has the right to bring life to an end.

II A twofold fault

The fault in suicide is twofold. It involves a running away from life, and it involves, as Thomas Aquinas saw, the usurpation of that which should belong to God alone. In that act man tries to escape from life by taking the times and seasons of life into his own hands.

III No condemnation

If there is one place where condemnation should be silent, and where sympathy should be paramount,

and where self-condemnation should
be in the heart, it is here. The man
who commits suicide does so because
he finds life intolerable and it may be,
it often is, the case that that is so
because no one helped to make it
tolerable for him. It might well be true
to say that there would be no suicides
if there had been people to whom the
person intent on suicide could have
unfolded his mind and heart. And
when people are defeated by life then
we may leave them with trust to the
mercy of God.

AUGUSTINE

*Augustine forbade suicide on
two grounds.*

*First, it is a step which in
the very nature of things
precludes repentance.*

*Second, it is murder, being a
breach of this sixth
commandment.*

CONCLUSION

For the Christian the taking of one's life is forbidden, but
we must regard with nothing but loving sympathy the
man who in his loneliness and lostness seeks this final way
of escape.

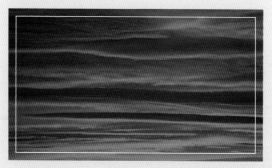

THE "JUST WAR"

CHRISTIAN LOVE

In our approach to this question we can only begin from
one place — we must begin from the conception of
Christian love. Christian love can act, and Christian love
can use force. But, if the Christian exercises force, that
force must have three characteristics.

I It must be remedial
It must be exercised with the single
idea of making the wrong-doer a
better man.

II It must be individual
It must be directed against the person
who has done the wrong.

III It must be exercised in love
It must be cleansed of hatred and of
bitterness and of malevolence. Its desire
is not for revenge.

ARGUMENTS AGAINST THE PACIFIST POSITION

I Public and private ethics

It is argued that the Christian Ethic of love is an
individual ethic of personal relationships between
individual people, and that it was not, and is not, meant to
govern the relationships of governments and states. This
argument says that as individuals we must in the spiritual
realm commit ourselves to the ethics of love, but as
citizens of the state our law is the law of the state, and we
must accept it.

Reply: And that is the argument on the basis of which at least a part of the German Church was able to accept Hitler.

II Perfection is impossible

There is the argument that we cannot look for, or even aim at, perfection, because we are living in a constricting situation. In other words, it is argued that since we are involved in a situation, we can only be as Christian as the situation will allow us to be. What we have to choose very often is the lesser of two evils. So, it is argued, there may arise situations in which war is the lesser of two evils.

Reply: It is possible to refuse to accept unchristian things, even if my refusal to accept them means some kind of martyrdom for me. It is only by refusing to accept the situation that in the end we can change the situation.

III Where war is not declared

What happens if in certain circumstances a state does not go to war?

Reply: At first sight this is a compelling argument, but there is a very real sense in which it is the supreme argument of unbelief. Do we really believe that Christianity will perish, unless it is defended by war? Do we really believe that it is possible to destroy the Christian faith?

If we really believe in Christianity we would also believe that Christianity is its own defense, and it may be that we must conclude that a faith which needs a defense of modern warfare is not a faith which even deserves to survive.

CHAPTER SEVEN

The Seventh Commandment

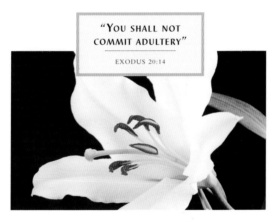

> ## "YOU SHALL NOT COMMIT ADULTERY"
>
> EXODUS 20:14

MEN, WOMEN AND GOD

It is a paradox of human nature that there was no sin regarded in Judaism with greater horror than adultery, and there was no sin which, to judge by the rebukes of the sages and prophets, was more common.

"He who commits adultery," said the Sage, "has no sense; he who does it destroys himself" (Proverbs 6:32).

JEREMIAH REBUKES ADULTERY

The horror that attached to the sin of adultery did not stop its committal. Jeremiah *(5:7, 8)* writes:

How can I pardon you?
Your children have forsaken me, and have sworn by those who are no gods.
When I fed them to the full, they committed adultery and trooped to the houses of harlots.
They were well-fed lusty stallions, each neighing for his neighbor's wife.

"Will you steal, murder, commit adultery, swear falsely, burn incense to Baal, and go after other gods than you have not known, and then come and stand before me in this house?" *(Jeremiah 7:9)*.

Again he says *(23:14)*:

But in the prophets of Jerusalem I have seen a horrible thing: they commit adultery and walk in lies.

CHASTITY

The seventh commandment deals with adultery, which is technically sexual intercourse of a woman with any other man than her husband; but we can hardly separate this from the larger issue of the whole question of sexual chastity. The wider word is fornication, which signifies sexual intercourse between unmarried persons, or of a married with an unmarried person.

The supreme importance that the Jewish mind attached to chastity can be seen from the passage in Deuteronomy which provides for the trial of a bride whom her husband suspects of not being a virgin at the time of her marriage, and for her death by stoning if the charge is proved to be true *(Deuteronomy 22:13-21)*.

Israel surrounded by impurity

All around Israel there was the worship of the power of reproduction.

❖ In *Deuteronomy 23:17, 18* the use of cult prostitutes is forbidden.
❖ They were there in the days of Rehoboam *(1 Kings 14:24).*
❖ Asa put them away *(1 Kings 15:12).*
❖ Josiah took steps against them *(2 Kings 23:7).*

The wonder was not that sometimes the Jews drifted into sexual irregularity; the miracle is that in such an environment the ideal of disciplined chastity ever came into being at all.

Marriage in the Jewish world

The seventh commandment invites us to look at the whole question of marriage and of the relationship between the sexes.

In Judaism the relationship between husband and wife had a very high ideal.

A SACRED OBLIGATION

To a Jew marriage was a sacred obligation. God had said: "Be fruitful and multiply, (GENESIS 1:28)

"It was to be inhabited that God formed the earth." (ISAIAH 45:18)

"It was not good for man to be alone." (GENESIS 2:18)

I There is the ideal of purity
"Immorality in the house is like a worm in vegetables" (Sotah 3b).

II There is the ideal of honor
The good man *"loves his wife more than himself"* and *"honours her more than himself"* (Yebamoth 62b).

III There is the ideal of considerateness
There was a proverb, *"If your wife is*

short, bend down and whisper to her" (Baba Matzia 59a).

IV There is the ideal of love

"When a man's first wife dies during his lifetime, it is as if the Temple had been destroyed in his lifetime. The world becomes dark for him" (Sanhedrin 22a). The ideal was the love that issues in care and consideration between husband and wife in all things.

CHRISTIANS LIVING SURROUNDED BY IMMORALITY

Christianity confronted that immorality with an uncompromising demand for purity.

❖ Immorality and all impurity were not even to be named among Christians.
❖ There was to be no filthiness.
❖ An immoral or impure man has no share in the kingdom of Christ and God *(Ephesians 5:3-20)*.
❖ Immorality, impurity, passion, evil desire must be inwardly put to death *(Colossians 3:5, 6)*.
❖ It is only the pure in heart, and therefore the pure in life, who see God *(Matthew 5:8)*.

RESPECT FOR THE BODY

We must begin with the simple fact that the Christian respected the body. To the Greek the body was no more than the prison of the soul. The world at that time was deeply infected by Gnostic thought, which believed that only spirit is good and that all matter is incurably evil.

But the Christian came with a new concept of the body. For the Christian the body is nothing less than the temple of the Holy Spirit *(1 Corinthians 3:16)*. If the body and all its functions offered to God, then immediately marriage becomes a sacred and holy state *(Hebrews 13:4)*.

New Testament teaching on marriage

There is clear and ample teaching about marriage in the New Testament. The most basic of all sayings is the saying which Jesus used: *"For this reason a man shall leave his father and mother and be joined to his wife, and the two shall become one" (Matthew 19:5; Mark 10:7; Genesis 1:27; 2:24).* This shows us two basic things about marriage.

I Separation

On the one hand marriage is separation. A man leaves his father and his mother. A person cannot continue to live the old life when he begins the new life. There is many a marriage spoiled because of the failure to realize this separation. The son or the daughter fails to realize that the center and the focus of life must be in the new home. The parent, and it is not unfair to say specially the mother, fails to realize that the son or the daughter has grown up, that there is a new set of loyalties and a new set of priorities.

II Union

But there is also union. The two who marry become one. There is more than one way of becoming one. There is the way of domination and abdication, the way in which one partner in the marriage becomes the absolutely dominating partner, until the personality of the other is more or less completely obliterated as an independent entity. That is certainly not the biblical way.

MAIN BIBLE PASSAGES

The chief biblical passages which deal with the relationship of husband and wife are:

- ❖ *Ephesians 5:21-33*
- ❖ *Colossians 3:18, 19*
- ❖ *1 Peter 3:1-7*
- ❖ *1 Timothy 2:9-15*
- ❖ *1 Corinthians 11:3*

Through all these passages there runs one principle which never varies. The principle of marriage is reciprocity. There is never a duty and never a privilege and never a responsibility that is all on one side. Every duty and every privilege is reciprocal.

A RECIPROCAL RELATIONSHIP

- ❖ Wives are to be subject to their husbands, but the husband must love his wife as Christ loves the Church *(Ephesians 5:23)*.
- ❖ The wife must respect the husband, but the husband must love the wife as he loves himself *(Ephesians 5:33)*.
- ❖ The wife must be submissive, but the husband must be considerate, for the wife is the weaker vessel *(1 Peter 3:7)*.

DIVORCE

HOW SHOULD A CHRISTIAN VIEW DIVORCE?

We have now come to a question which is a real problem for the Christian Ethic, and it is a problem rendered doubly difficult by the fact that it is not only a theological problem, but also a human problem. What is the Christian attitude to divorce?

THE JEWISH AND GREEK BACKGROUND

Unquestionably, the Jewish ideal of marriage was very high, whatever the practice may have been.

Equally unquestionably, there was in the Hellenistic world of Greece and Rome an almost unparalleled laxity in sexual ethics, so that divorce was normal rather than exceptional.

It is clear that these two factors, apart from anything else, would combine to produce in the Christian Ethic an uncompromising demand. The uncompromising demand would be in line with the highest ideals of Judaism, and it would be an inevitable reaction against the shameless immorality of the pagan world.

Teaching against divorce

I Back to Moses

The Pharisees questioned Jesus as to the legality of
divorce. He asked them what Moses himself had said
about it. They replied that Moses was no more than a
concession to the hardness of the hearts of the Jewish
people.

II Further back, to Genesis

Jesus then took the matter back behind Moses to the
Genesis story *(Genesis 2:24; 1:27)*, and to the saying that
for the sake of marriage a man would leave father and
mother and be joined to his wife, and that the union
would be one person. Therefore, said Jesus, what God has
joined man must not put asunder.

Matthew's addition

Matthew adds something still further to
this. According to Matthew when the
disciples heard this saying of Jesus, and
when they realized how absolutely
indissoluble Jesus believed marriage to
be, they said that, if this was the case, it
was surely better not to marry at all.

Jesus' answer

Jesus' answer was: *"Not all men can
receive this precept, but only those to whom
it is given"*, or, as the NEB has it,
*"That is something which not everyone can
accept, but only those for whom God has
appointed it"* (Matthew 19:10, 11)

CHRISTIAN MARRIAGE IS FOR CHRISTIANS

*That is to say, the
acceptance of the absolute
prohibition of divorce is
something which not
everyone can accept. To put
this completely simply and
directly, it means that
Christian marriage is only
possible for a Christian. It is
only a Christian who can
understand and accept and
achieve the standards of
Christian marriage.*

SEX BEFORE MARRIAGE

THREE SITUATIONS

What about the question of sexual intercourse before marriage? There are three situations to consider:

I Anticipation

There is sexual intercourse by what we might call anticipation, where two people claim that they love each other so much, and that they are so certain to marry, that they can anticipate marriage by having sexual intercourse.

Reply: It would be equally possible to say that they love each other so much that they will not have sexual intercourse until they are totally and irrevocably committed to each other. Nothing is certain in this life, and it is not certain that they will marry.

II Trial

There is sexual intercourse for the reason of trial or experiment. Sometimes two people argue that they will not commit themselves to marriage until they find out by experiment whether or not they are suited to each other.

Reply: The error in that attitude is that it is not possible in that way to simulate the conditions of marriage.

III Living together
There is the case of those who choose to live together,
but who, as they say, see no necessity for any marriage
ceremony, either civil or religious.

Reply: At its very lowest marriage is a contract; and at its
highest marriage is a promise made in the presence of
God.

IT IS WRONG
The ultimate argument of the Christian must be, not that
such sexual intercourse is dangerous (although that may
be used as a secondary argument) but that it is wrong,
and, even if completely safe, it would still be wrong. What
then are the fundamental arguments against it?

I It shatters family life
If sexual intercourse before — and outside — marriage is
accepted as normal, then the whole institution of the
family is radically altered. The very essence of the family is
that in it two people take each other to have and to hold
all the days of their life. The stability of the home depends
on the exclusive relationship of the two people round
whom it revolves.

II It demands privileges without responsibilities
To demand pre-marital sexual intercourse is to demand
privilege without responsibility. It is to demand from
someone the gift of something which can never be
replaced without any corresponding acceptance of
responsibility for the welfare of the giver. For a woman to
surrender her virginity is for her to surrender something
which can never be replaced; she is a literally changed person.

HOMOSEXUALITY

We begin with the biblical attitude to this way of sex.

I Sodom
Genesis 19:1-11 gives the origin of the other name for homosexuality, sodomy. To Lot there came two angel visitors, but when he brought them into his house the men of Sodom surrounded it with threats and even with violence, demanding that the two visitors should be handed over to them to satisfy their lust. The story shows the loathing of Old Testament religion for it.

II Male prostitutes
The Old Testament has fairly frequent references to male prostitutes who were located in the temples of Baal.
- During the reign of Rehoboam *"there were also make cult prostitutes in the land" (1 Kings 14:24)*.
- Asa, as a good king, *"put away the male cult prostitutes out of the land" (1 Kings 15:12)*.

III. Homosexuality is condemned
Homosexuality is unsparingly condemned in the Old Testament. Leviticus says: *"You shall not lie with a male as with a woman; it is an abomination" (Leviticus 18:22)*. In the New Testament Paul cites homosexuality as part of the moral rot of the pagan world *(Romans 1:26, 27)*; and one of the sins from which the Christians have been saved and purified *(1 Corinthians 6:9)*.

THE WAY TO A SOLUTION

Whatever we say, we must say tentatively, not so much as a solution, as a sketch of the way to a solution.

I An abnormal condition
We have to begin with the admission that homosexuality is an abnormal condition. This has to be accepted first.

II Control is necessary
If it is an abnormal condition, the practices which it involves must be strictly controlled. It is not something which can be freely practiced or propagated.

III It must never be legalized
Where it is deliberate perversion involving deliberate corruption, it must never be legalized, and it must be dealt with like any other crime against society.

IV If homosexuality is part of a person's being
In this case three things may be said:

   i) The homosexual must be helped to see that his is an abnormal condition.

   ii) He must be persuaded that no one is condemning him for being as he is, but must be encouraged to seek a cure.

   iii) Already treatments exist.

V Do not be condemning
Homosexuals who associate for the only human relationship they know must be regarded with sympathy and those of us who have never known the problem must hesitate to condemn something outside our experience.

CONTRACEPTION

IS ANY METHOD OF CONTRACEPTION RIGHT FOR
THE CHRISTIAN?

Apart from anything else, the attitude of the Roman
Catholic Church, which opposes birth control by any
means of contraception, demands that we ask this
question.

I Is there more than one reason for sexual intercourse?

On only one ground can contraception be regarded as
essentially wrong. It is only wrong if the only function of
sexual intercourse is to produce a child. I do not think
that the view can be held. It is true that the ultimate
reason for the existence of the sex instinct is to ensure the
continuance of the race; but it is also true that sexual
intercourse is the deepest and the most fundamental
expression of love; it is literally consummation. It can
surely express the ultimate union of love as well as the
desire to beget a child.

II Controlling world population

There can be no doubt that the limitation of families is a
duty in a world which is in serious danger of over-
population. Some means of population limitation is
essential.

III The economic argument

There is no doubt that for parents to produce more
children than they can provide with a proper chance in
life is an act of grave irresponsibility. The limitation of the
family to the number which we can afford is reasonable.

IV Opening the door to immorality

To provide the means of contraception and to approve of them has in this and every generation been declared to be an opening of the door to immorality. It has simply to be answered that any drug and any process can be misused; but that is no reason for not using it at all. If everything in life which has a risk in it was removed, there would be very little left. But it is to be laid down for the Christian Ethic that contraception must be within marriage.

V Guard against selfishness

The one thing which we must guard against is a purely selfish limitation of the family. A limitation of the family in the interests of increased luxury and increased "freedom" is a selfish thing, and therefore a wrong thing.

CONCLUSION

On balance it may well be that we should thank God for the scientific and medical discoveries which have made possible both family planning and the expression of love.

CHAPTER EIGHT

The Eighth Commandment

> ### "YOU SHALL
> ### NOT STEAL"
>
> EXODUS 20:14

THE CONDEMNATION
OF THE THIEF

THEFTS OF NON-MATERIAL THINGS

This is what might be called a basic commandment. It is not only a necessary part of the Christian Ethic; it is a necessary part of any agreement to live together. It is part of the foundations of any society, and without obedience to it any society would be impossible.

TYPES OF THEFT

There are thefts other than the theft of material things,
and many a person who would never be guilty of material
theft is frequently guilty of them, and they are such that
they are the most serious thefts of all.

I Time

There is the theft of time. When a man enters into
employment, he also enters into a contract, be it written
or be it understood, in which he undertakes to give his
employer so much of his time in return for so much pay.
He may, for instance, engage to work for eight hours a
day. It may well be that of all thefts the theft of time is
most common.

There are few people who are not guilty of the theft
of time and of effort from the people to whom they have
contracted to give their time and effort.

II Innocence

There is such a thing as the theft of innocence. There is a
kind of person who seduces others into sin. When Robert
Burns went as a young man to Irvine to learn flax-
dressing, he fell in with a certain man who taught him a
good deal about reckless living. Afterwards Burns said of
him: *"His friendship did me a mischief."* There are those
whose alleged friendship does others a mischief.

III Character or good name

There is such a thing as the theft of a person's character or
good name. The recklessness with which people repeat
stories about other people without ever checking them is
an astonishing thing. To listen to the malicious story is
almost, if not quite, as bad as to repeat it.

Is all private property theft?

It has sometimes been said that all private property is
theft. But private property is not in the least wrong, when
the owner of it remembers that he possesses it, not only to
use it for himself, but also to use it for others.

But private property is a kind of theft when a man
uses it for nothing but his own pleasure and his own
gratification, with never a thought for anyone else. It is
not the property but the selfishness which constitutes the
theft.

THREE OTHER TYPES
OF THEFT

There are other things which arise in
the day-to-day dealing of men with
each other which are in effect theft.

I Debt

In the first place there is debt. *"Owe no
one anything,"* says Paul
(Romans 13:8), and that is in fact a
Christian principle. Debt is theft in
this sense — it is a withholding from a
man that which is his due. There may
be times when this is not fatally
serious; but it happens again and again
in modern circumstances that a small
tradesman has been driven out of
business because there are customers
who will not pay their debts.

The state of society is such that
debt as a kind of theft needs to be
stressed.

AN EXAMPLE FROM
THE BIBLE

*The Bible is always
supremely interested in the
rights of the man for whom
life is a struggle. Twice the
Bible lays down the rights of
such a man.*

**"You shall not oppress a
hired servant who is poor
and needy, ... you shall
give him his hire on the
day he earn it, before the
sun goes down (for he is
poor, and sets his heart
upon it); lest he cry
against you to the Lord,
and it be sin in you."**

DEUTERONOMY 24:14-15

II Lending money in the wrong way

The Old Testament contains a three times repeated prohibition on lending money at interest, at least to a fellow Jew.

I) EXODUS 22:25

"If you lend money to any of my people with you who is poor, you shall not be to him as a creditor, and you shall not exact interest from him."

II) LEVITICUS 25:37-37

"Take no interest from him (that is, your brother who is in poverty) or increase, but fear your God; that your brother may live beside you. You shall not lend him money at interest, nor give him your food for profit."

III) DEUTERONOMY 23:19

"You shall not lend upon interest to your brother."
The law of the Bible is that no one must ever take advantage of another's need, and use that need for his own profit and enrichment.

III Just scales and balances

A further repeated commandment is have just scales, balances and measurements. We get it in *Leviticus 19:35-36: "You shall do no wrong in judgment, in measures of length or weight or quantity. You shall have just balances, just weights, a just ephah, and a just hin."*

Careful justice and meticulous honesty in these things is the natural and essential expression of true religion.

CHAPTER NINE
The Ninth Commandment

> **"YOU SHALL NOT BEAR FALSE WITNESS AGAINST YOUR NEIGHBOR"**
>
> EXODUS 20:16

THE TRUTH, THE WHOLE TRUTH, AND NOTHING BUT THE TRUTH

The ninth commandment runs: *"You shall not bear false witness against your neighbor" (Exodus 20:16)*, and it is repeated in *Deuteronomy 5:20*.

THE EXODUS AND THE DEUTERONOMY VERSIONS

Although the English form is in both cases false witness, the Hebrew is different. In Exodus the meaning is lying or untrue; in Deuteronomy the meaning is insincere, empty, frivolous. The meaning is not essentially different, but the Exodus version concerns the nature of the evidence while Deuteronomy emphasises the spirit in which it is given.

SEVEN EXAMPLES OF FALSENESS

False witness is a lie, to be seen in the context of the attitude of the Bible to lies and to falsehood.

I Hosea and Jeremiah
Hosea condemns it. "You have ploughed iniquity, you have reaped injustice, you have eaten the fruit of lies" *(Hosea 10:13)*. So does Jeremiah: *"They bend their tongue like a bow; falsehood and not truth has grown strong in the land" (Jeremiah 9:3)*.

II Lying can become ingrained
Lying can become ingrained. The wicked may well say: *"we have made lies our refuge, and in falsehood we have taken shelter" (Isaiah 28:15)*.

III Lying ends in delusion
The result is delusion and loss of way. *"You have uttered delusions and seen lies,"* says Ezekiel *(13:8)*.

IV What is linked to lying
It is interesting and significant to see the things in company with which lying is associated.

❖ *"they multiply falsehood and violence" (Hosea 12:1)*.
❖ *Jerusalem is full of lies and booty, or plunder (Nahum 3:1)*.
❖ *False prophets commit adultery and walk in lies (Jeremiah 23:14)*.

V Lying is a sin which profanes God
They profane God by lying and listening to lies *(Ezekiel 13:17-19)*. The Psalmist has the vivid phrase: *"The godless besmear me with lies" (Psalm 119:69)*.

VI Warnings against falsehood
Falsehood and lying will be exposed. *Isaiah 28:17* says:
*"Hail will sweep away the refuge of lies, and water will
overwhelm the shelter."*

VII The prayer of the wise
Note that the prayer of the wise man: *"Remove far from me
falsehood and lying"* (Proverbs 30:8).

WHAT CAUSES LYING?

I Malice
In Exodus there is the injunction *(23:1)*: *"you shall not
utter a false report. You shall not join hands with a wicked man,
to be a malicious witness."* There is nothing commoner than
the story maliciously repeated, or invented.

II The lie of fear
Perhaps the first and commonest of lies, is the lie of fear,
to escape the consequences of what we have done. This is

the kind of lie we begin to tell in childhood and go on telling all our lives. This kind of lie will sooner or later catch up with us. *"Be sure,"* said Moses, *"your sin will find you out"* (Numbers 32:23).

III The lie of carelessness
A man can become almost chronically inaccurate in his statements, not so much deliberately as carelessly.

IV The lie for profit
This is the kind of lie at which the high-pressure salesman is adept, and of which so much advertising is an example. Allied with this is the lie of propaganda, made by a person or party to win support. In war *"truth is the first casualty"*.

V The lie of silence
Silence – the coward's refuge – can often be a lie.

VI The lie which is a half-truth
It is easy to give the truth a twist to suit ourselves. A half-truth is often more dangerous than an out-and-out falsehood.

VII The lie to self
There is no harder thing than to be strictly honest with oneself. Burns prayed to see ourselves as others see us.

VIII The lie of boasting
One of the hardest truths to tell is that about ourselves.

IX The lie to God
We can lie to God by trying to conceal things from him. But He hears our words and sees our deeds.

CHAPTER TEN

The Tenth Commandment

"YOU SHALL NOT
COVET YOUR
NEIGHBOR'S HOUSE;
YOU SHALL NOT COVET
YOUR NEIGHBOR'S
WIFE, OR HIS
MANSERVANT OR HIS
MAIDSERVANT, OR HIS
OX, OR HIS ASS, OR
ANYTHING THAT IS
YOUR NEIGHBOR'S"

(EXODUS 20:17;
DEUTERONOMY 5:21)

THE WRONG DESIRE

INNER THOUGHTS

With the tenth commandment the
commandments enter a new world.
Up to now the commandments have
dealt with outward actions; but this
commandment deals with inner thoughts.

This commandment lays by far the hardest task upon
man. To control one's actions is one thing. To control one's
thoughts and feelings and emotions is quite another.

COVETOUSNESS IN ACTION

We must look at the areas of life in which covetousness

operates, and at the things which men desire, when they have no right to desire them.

I Material things

The simplest form of covetousness is for material things, for money and for the things which money can buy. The Bible is never in any doubt that the love of money is the root of all evils *(1 Timothy 6:10)*.

When acquisitiveness gets out of proportion, then it becomes covetousness and then it is wrong.

❖ Covetousness can lead to dishonesty.
❖ Covetousness can lead to exploitation.
❖ Covetousness is at the root of the gambling fever which has society in its grip.

II Status and place

There is the covetousness for status and place. Jesus knew how this desire was part of human nature, especially in the scribes and the Pharisees of his day, although not only in them *(Matthew 23;5-7; Mark 12:38-39; Luke 11;43; 14:7-11; 20:46)*. It is an odd fact that there is no place where this is more common than within the Church.

III People

A very serious form is the covetousness for people. The commandment forbids a man to covet his neighbor's wife; the Deuteronomy version of the commandment *(5:21)* puts that at the head of the forbidden things.

And Jesus in the Sermon on the Mount forbids the look of lustful desire *(Matthew 5:7)*. It is the kind of covetousness which produced David's illicit love for Bathsheba *(2 Samuel 11)*.

IV Idolatry

The last word about covetousness as a quality is said in the Letter to the Colossians *(3:5)*, for there covetousness is identified with idolatry. Idolatry means putting something else in the position which God alone should occupy. But the heart that is occupied with God will banish all false loves, whatever they may be.

THE ROOTS OF COVETOUSNESS

Now we turn to see just what the roots and the foundations of covetousness are, for we are better able to avoid a physical or a spiritual illness if we know its basic conditions.

I The quest for happiness

The basis and foundation of covetousness is the idea that to get what we have not got will bring happiness. The feeling in the mind and heart is: *"If I had this or that, I would be happy. If only I could get this or that I would be satisfied."* But covetousness cannot be satisfied by acquisition of anything; it can only be cured when the desire to acquire is eliminated.

II Things bring happiness

We could put this another way: *covetousness comes from the idea that things can bring happiness.*

If the possession of things brought happiness then this would be the happiest and most contented age in history, for never was there such material well-being. Things which were once the possession of the privileged few are now the possession of many — which in itself is an excellent thing; but it is also true that there never was a

more neurotic and dissatisfied age in history. Unrest and unease are the marks of the affluent society.

III The covetousness for a person

The covetousness for a person, the desire for someone whom we should not desire, who does not and who ought not to belong to us. Here the feeling is that, if we could only possess the person who is forbidden to us, then happiness would come. Suppose we take the person whom we ought not to take. There may be the thrill of the moment. But unless a man is lost to conscience, there can be no ultimate happiness that way.

- ❖ If it is kept secret, there is the constant fear of discovery, which in the end poisons the pleasure.
- ❖ If the thing is openly admitted, the memory of the other people who have been involved in the situation, the thought of their shame and their sorrow, the memory of how they have been wronged, is always in the background, and when passion dies and there is time for thought, there can be no happiness in a situation which has caused someone else's tragedy.

CONTENTMENT

I How contentment is lost
    i) Any situation which causes a man to lose his self-respect or which involves him in his own self-condemnation, cannot be productive of happiness.
    ii) Any forbidden relationship, which requires concealment, or which is the cause of tragedy for others, cannot be productive of happiness.
    iii) Anything which estranges a man from God, and which he would wish to hide from God, cannot be productive of happiness.

II How contentment is found
There are three things which lead to perfect satisfaction, perfect happiness and perfect contentment.
    i) In regard to oneself contentment is found in the self-respect that will not stoop to that which is low.
    ii) In regard to our fellowmen contentment is found in the love which is for ever pure and faithful.
    iii) In regard to God contentment is found in the love which issues in true obedience, given not in the fear of God, but in the love of God.
    If a man's life has these three things, he will covet nothing for there will be nothing to desire that he does not possess.